FUSTIAN

RACONTEUR'S RANTS

YASHVEER VATS GAURAV

Made with ♥ on the Notion Press Platform
www.notionpress.com

Contents

Contents

Contents

1. Melody of artery

I came across her secrets at a cave full of treasures trying to find something that could fill up the void of voices with me, the echos wouldn't stop the murmurs wouldn't go away, and as I whispered to find the crystals that carried the songs of centuries if not millennia. Filled with a book that was written with ink made from tears, so many. I struggled to find the voices that could shun my own and I struggled to locate mysteries that weren't and that's when I found a gem. It was born from the fire of the sea that couldn't thrash and it was molten by the sky to the shape of a pandemonium.

A girl was floating behind it to keep it hidden and to keep to the flowers she grew, to the birds she sang with to the bones of the dead and the wings of fates she knew she could earn it all but she kept it to herself. A gift that was seen by everyone but her. Everyone but the sun-kissed skin and mystique hair, with the golden eyes and the pink muster lips. She felt godly but she didn't want to be divine. But even divinity praised that gem of voice.

2. Nubivagant

She feels like clouds,
She's always on a trip from one lane to the other
and we glare always at the sights we see of the eyes that meet.
That sketchbook in her hands
That favorite pen She has
Her hair smells of jasmine
I don't know if I know too much or she's just so charming
I know she's destined for the lights
Museum walls look like art in her eyes
I know she'll bring the colors to life
Knowing every inch of her startles in the sky
Was she painted on clouds?
By sunlight and rain
Was she distanced hills
That is sealed with plains
I hope it takes a little while
For the thunders to barge in
How her acrylics can be held
In my hands like she did
I hope she twists the sights
Hold my hand within hers tight
The closest thing to anything
I've seen immortal life

Wish she'd think of me the same
But I'm just a poet who's far far away
I hope she burns away the skies
Rains have loved me always so it's a sweet sight
I hope she kills me from within
So my memories of loving her stay's always thin
I hope she hates me to goodbye
Bec ause I was never made to see stars with her in the same sky

3. Gilded Dances

Dancing with you
On a white line
The fate thread is black
But your eyes are bright
I know things are cracked
Life has been fiend
Philophobia whelves
On your destiny
Tell me I'm wrong
That this one dance you take
You feel at home but
I'm just hiraeth
Cruor love stamps
Tattoo'd on skin
Life's been unfair
And I know the gild
The golden gleemshine
That's on your lips
Deserving a romance
That's not paper thin

4. Romance-less Love

I fell into the lakes of limbo, in the fog of the dark, and my eyes somewhat knew my existence is already on an edge. The rubrics of life were dependent on the material of the lake but the lake is a mirror where you can pass, but there are people outside the lake who won't harm you but talk you out of it, they say it's not worth it and I was never loved, that a place where I know I'm unloved is better than a place where being loved is folklore amongst the world and the world runs around the brightest thing in the system and I know my heart is being unswerving every inch by second. With a million strings attached, the voices cut like scissors.

Every name unthreads itself like it was never real but there is one string that's so pale I can see the moon through it. It drags down to the right side up to where a romanceless lover washes her hair thinking maybe it's the last day she'll ever witness the eyes of the guilty, the one loved with songs and the one filled with sorrows. The thread is on her fingertips and she fiddles with it like a child she leans in to tie a knot she feels her eyes melt on sight. The strings down to hellboundscapes and she knows that breath is the last. One pull from the gilded string and I'm out of limbo from hours. It took one pull to save me just one string of love, the

first and the last time my savior wasn't a word.

5. Five Houses

And how I met her 5 houses across mine, yelling her name as I watched her walk by. I made friends with her and I was proud of it, a friend that isn't judgmental yet honest. Someone you don't need to rely on but still understand and it got to a point I thought
"This is the time, I'll have my teenage life!"
Oh, how I thought that, I thought I have a party friend. I thought I'd need to buy 2 concert tickets from now on, how I'd always visit events with a friend and I'd have hangovers at houses and I'd share all my secrets, she was a friend but even more, she was a journey to a life I craved but never knew how to enter.
And an apology did more than enough when I picked her up by the gully guys didn't it? I always knew life works in its odd ways and for the break my unhinged self was it, the break was more than a breakup than a break but to some extent, I knew I was overreacting so I left it be, and let it be that corner of unconscious platonic romances I killed because I was too scared to speak. And when she sat in my car and thanked me for it, it was almost like I was forgiven for sins I never committed, my relief felt so honest. You know she's odd and weird and that kinda makes it safer to be with

her because I'm the same. We are a year apart or maybe two at most but she seems so much like someone I've known for a while even tho we've met like 7 times. It feels the same. Her radiance is never unseen, somehow a role model not even exaggerating. She glows like a light in the aether yet her shadow finds a way to sneak in. The locks in her mind don't have keys they have codes and the codes are displaced within a wall I cannot reach, maybe I don't want to at this point. My point of view of hers is pretty enough to light up the edges and the room as long as it's empty it has enough space to balter.

6. Bollywood Compliments

"Everyone leaves me when they're in love" I know this, but then On the edge of the unimaginable world I heard
"thank god I'm not in love"
Sounded like a song from a 70's Bollywood movie, the charm of the linguistic code that literature defines this paragraph to be is so vaguely lovable, the idea that someone's glad that she hasn't felt the most beautiful thing In the world just because she hasn't left my side felt like a shot in the head, as if every loveless scar was fixed by a single bandaid, that too was like pretty for its own self because it makes me want to dance along the lines of her name but I know if I dance with an injury I'll get worse but I know for a fact if I fall she'll pick me, if I don't bleed she'd still lay with me and if I wither she'd collect my petals. Every word of her sounds closer to Bombay.

7. Fiesty

And she Danced at the edge of insanity
I thought to myself
"Isn't it risky to be this carefree"
But how do you live when you don't see the sea?
And I saw her eyes shine at me
"What a flirt," I thought
Knowing my mind lives on satire
And her's lives on relief
She felt like the stars
when she laid her head on me
I glanced at her knowing what she'd say
"It's funny for them to burn from jealousy" and I agree
And the wind has burnt a thousand times
And a thousand lakes have been dried
And the swords have flung on throats behalf
And we still hold hands, sometimes but tight.
She's still a secret best friend of mine
She's still the princess of spring hills
No matter how tall I am
Even with height, her level won't work for me with stilts

8. Garden of Sorrows

The way my fingertips feel on my chest makes me want to weep, the way my skin crawls with Dislike, the way my fingers are ripped the way my elbows have a bump the way my face is filled with acne the way my under eyes carries my whole face, the way I'm never able to sleep without crying the way I'm just justifying my suffering that I deserve it but do I? Seeing all the people make videos with their friends, hanging out being all bright while I'm locked in a cage I can't wait to get out of. The way my heart goes blunt when I see lovers, the way whenever I fall in love I make myself feel unworthy, and the way everyone I talk to I give my best because I know I'm not their favorite, it's hard to be anyone's favorite when you're as undesirable as a plucked flower. Maybe you're pretty and maybe you're capable to be great but to a tree that has millions of more flowers you're nothing,

all I am is a sight withered to stay unconscious because if I gain myself, love, will I even be considered worthy of a petal? I hate to be a hater but I can't help myself but feel I'm a weight on the clouds that support the Gardens of lovers. Maybe if I rain down I'll finally be one with the ground.

9. Find you someday

The night has been mourning
The way you sound
The whistles tune themselves
To sing just like you
Just like autumn
I feel like a new start
Just like spring
You pluck my heart apart
The days have gotten longer
The love potion stays stronger
A hand in hand is a wish I hold
My heart on dance with your show
Just like autumn
I'm bilateral like our hearts
Just like spring
You've made us feel sophrosyne
The psychomachy of war
Of weather, it's you or me
That's on the edge of love
Or am I just too blind to see?
My eyes represent autumn
By its velvet browns
Your eyes represent spring

By the miraculous ardor
"Vestigo sight arcane belamour
Bator thy soul comesation
Defiance of Bonhomie lover
Mauvis arrives doorstep"-
[Follow your mysterious lover
And your soul might burn
But defy your destiny with them
And Darkness will haunt forever]
Because my heart is a fowl
And your distance is an aviary
The reasoning of your sea-deep eyes
Says maybe I'll find you at the seiche

10. Pretentious fools

My fingertips, on her mists
I think she needs a hand to hold on to.
We are pretentious fools
Looking for love but thinking
we've got what we've been aiming for
I see her face, in badminton plays
She looks like she'd fall for boys older age
She'd see me as. Someone who'd pass
And I'm grateful that feelings gonna last
I wish she saw, the same old girl
Who thinks she's worth it
With no changing bits, No sweater slits.
Just nail paint on our mindless whists
She walks across, this empty hall
Finding printouts as memories
I hope she knows, that every chore
Doesn't need to feel like the enemy
She'd cry in arms, the rightful ones
Where they feel it was waiting as
She's pretty seen, very keen
On finding everything she'd ever want for her
She sits across, this empty lawn
I hope she mows that grass

Because her dreams, stay afreen
If She'd let it grow back then
Plant a seed, grow orchids
Maybe you need rest to feel yourself
Just know you'll stay, on empty lanes
If you let the future be afraid
I'd stand beside. In your dorm of time
Yet I won't speak a word for you
You know your worth, you know your work
Just what we are supposed to

11. Voids

I can see the hollow in you
Which I cannot fill
I can see you waiting
For someone to awaken
I can see your masks
I can see your scars
I can see your pretty face
I can see your dreams
Yet I keep quiet
I can’t hold your hand
I wish I could fix the dead loads
I wish I could turn it into the sand
I’ve loved you for a while
And I look at the land and the sky
Yet never did I see
Someone prettier Than you
I'm not in love
I’ve just loved you
The way you talk the way you see
The way the world isn’t what’s meant to be
It’s me wanting to
hold your hand
And go to cafes

To talk about crushes
To laugh in subways
And I've seen you wonder
The lakes of empty cities
Knowing I could just be happy
Watching you be someone to me

12. Browns

And I gazed at the browns in the soil, in her eyes, on her lips and I can never get tired of it because after all, it's my favorite color. The brunette hair looks black unless it's under sunlight those fingertips that paint inside a room have so much passion it makes the air clear like we are in the open sky and I've never felt such admiration for an artist. "Lacuna lucent sweven Noceur nocturnal eesome"
A phrase I made up while at her sight, it means the missing void of a vision that even night doesn't sleep to see. I'm the moon after all and the night is my blanket

,

I'd ice the earth to Neptune if it meant I couldsee her eyes for eternity.

13. Atelier

The atelier of fates
Where our string was destined
I wanna visit the station where
The artists are resting
And while the finger sewed around
Resting on the anodyne guitar
I'm just in questions of how
You could be that far
The empyrean voice that stands up to calm
Sounds like your artist lived in the lake of siren yard
Hands filled with nubivagant ink
Looks like you were my muse always meant to be
And I wither, I do
But I hear every song of you
Tenebrose bones and sussurus love
Turn into my amorist tones

14. Fortnight

It's a fortnight left to demise, do you feel autumn would leave me just like they did? I've always hated October's but the lush brown hair that was lit on fire and ashed to black is now growing Grasps again. It never feels like me to be slithering on raw seas made of clots, is it? The questions I ask are paray you. Because the answers don't exist in a word or a sentence. They exist in a judgment of how much you trust me, and your fear of losing me. The flickering crystals lent on my eyes shine like the moon when they're touched with love but the same crystals melt to tears that can be acid for your skin if touched with hurt and I crave the day my demise is lunisolace and all the people who've called me liars were hence proved right.
I wish I was a liar, rather than a dead man
But if I live this October I'll be neither of those again
"I hope you stay some more Octobers"
I wish I was kissed with this sentence, to be truly sun-kissed
And every word of lips is vanilla lisps
I still want to hear the honey tied up my earrings
But the girl in red will never sound the same for neither of yours serene

15. Eyes for Asthetes

Enchanted voice of yours
I still walk on the floors
Where the land is made of pure
Purissima and white rose
The leaves have fallen up
The gravity's not holding on
Do I pull back
Or do I pull forth?
My eyes stare every way
Just to find you stray away
So close to grasping yours to be
I just see a serien
Guitarists and their spells
To make hollow things
Feel echoingly, maybe that's why
I fall for them
Vernorexia of the blue
Sinking me into the hue
The colors are still on to who
When your string's in the sew
Star kiss on a Standing shore
Jupiter's June on the Moon
Impossible things done to be

Made it feel maroon
Vines on the wallpaper
I can only see our faces
Looking at each other
With a million stances
Broken mirrors with Kashmir tea
The heart and its unpolluted destiny
Light mint eyes with mascara
Eyes just made for the aesthetes

16. Sixteen

Every day, I pass by her. Saying hi from the back of the crook of her neck always gets her by surprise. I don't know what it is but her reactions always look like "he's so weird" and that brings a smile to me, I wonder if she thinks about me. I wonder if she even acknowledges my existence after we're all at home. She's gorgeous like lotuses, I see flowers all around her. She's such a Cliche for me, I love cliches because you know your heart has seen something closer to the things shown on television than on the realistic affairs of a loveless memory. To be sixteen has never felt so pretty without her.

17. Siren Yard

And the siren yard
Still weaves your fate
And the ringing of night
Falls deep aside, on your shoulder
When the sky rests on the stars
And the stars rest selene
Do you know who the Cresent
Lays her eyes on?
And while the Glistening aura
Sweeps your mind
Do you feel the breeze
Of the resting incline
As it follows your freckled neck
Through the cloud skies
The immensity of the awknologed
Do you feel its light suffice?
The resting bel amour is light
Yet the mystics they sleep
That one mirror of truth yet
Now just shows your smile
The Cresent is still a blanket
So it could rest the earth
The candles slept to the cool

But the silver silt still issues
So darling darling fall asleep
It's five past one
I know these rhythms keep you tied
But life's only begun

18. Coddeled

And when I balter with the wind
And spring along valleys
The wet leaves sonder of monsoon rains
I feel the night collide
The moon holds the sun
The birds sing Beethoven
The stars coded with demise
They begin to speak with the rain
The frogs coddled in blankets
The fungus grew to shelter the cats
The mesmerized butterflies
Resting of the feline's tail
She's happy, she's smiling
The raindrops are tears of her embrace
I feel her skin soft siren songs
And I feel the comfort that I'm where she belongs

19. Wilted Dandelions

And I can see her eyes wilt like dandelions, going blind at the sight of me. I can see all around yet I only find one thing that startles me: that love isn't real? It's too good to be real? Yet I believe it is, why's it so hard to be loved but so easy to love? Was I made to be a flower in the garden of weeds because it seems like I'm only loving myself and everyone else until my heart shatters? I wish my eyes wilt like dandelions too.

20. Bolide

And I feel the chevelure startle the sight of my rings as I whist upon my wrongful judgment within, I've walked on thin ice on the cased-up shores of seas and tides and so many coasts. I feel like a god now that I've killed enough eyes but I drill upon that idea that I have to be right and I trust me to trust you when you tell me you're lying but even the truth hides from these indecent eyes. I've wished her away too many times to have been considered an honorable ally but I know I've fucked it up too many times. She looks out for me and thinks for me nice but I have that feeling that it'll go to an ecliptic moonrise, I've bled every mirror to tell me what'd be right but maybe it's regret that's keeping me up her eyes. I love her so much but I hate that height, that "fake it till you make it" bullshit I despise. Do you look at the stars to make you feel like it's a lie? Maybe I'd not fight this feeling to be right. I've seen enough justice to let the high priestess be and yet all I feel is a shame for being a unblind eye shriek. I'm bound to make secrets and call them mistakes, if I didn't read people maybe this wouldn't have gone that way. If only my love for her outweighs my hate. Would she still love me if she read this with my name?

21. 21st may

The morning of the 21st may
The first glance on your face
And I sonder to your vision
With windows that you let stay
I've been here since October
I've witnessed the kashmir
The paper hearts in my soul
And the midnight memories
And the forsaken moon dawned
Your hustling morning
To Geminis in forever your
Heart's alluring
While I stay here reminiscent
To your belonging in a book
You seem to be so unreal
You seem to be unlooked
I've read a billion faces
I've met a million seas
I've seen drops of me
I've yet to grasp your winds
And I've heard you go about
Music, voices, and feels
I've felt the comfort in your throat

That I've never felt on the beach
And I tell you, you sound like a forest
A soul old as the sea
When I look into your eyes I can only see a garden
Because you border the feels
It's the day when you risked up
On the first touch of light
To forever when the fire burns
I hope you stay on this side

22. Lovers?

As I sit with her on the chair, waiting for her to touch my fingertips I wonder what the tulips on her nail polish would look like, what'd be the letters sent to me when I'm finally in her arms. Would they be of Jealousy? But the fire of deserving burns more in me than them. I hate her yet I'd love to be hers, I just want to be sown in her ribs with silk of tenebrific tenets. She carries serpents around her lakes and I still dive into them, she never tells me to stop because she's been a spectator since. She's just always been there, watching me, growing up with me yet it's scary that she's been with me and never held my hand. I wonder if I'm just someone she made up as a friend, a folie à deux maybe. But once our hands are held many will cry and weep.
So many of my friends wanted to be hers
Yet they cry because they wanted to have me
Maybe everyone else had their metanoia, everyone but me.
So she'll kiss my lips and seal my breath with the lock of our palms.

She's death, after all

23. Choir

The songs of heal were sung by the sirens where I stayed for hours of eight, the choir felt like a boon on my mind. I saw every word tuned off the lips of the chanteuse waiting to strike. Then I had a glare of this rustic art of a room where every tie knotted the heads and every lisp would've had you dead.

I saw an olden, someone I knew and probably despised but for war, the enemy of your enemy is a friend. Amends were made, and loose ends tied, I don't exactly know what bloomed between her and me but I created a dynamic of Rivalry. Beloved Rivalry that'll probably be a significance lighter than hatred.

A room of singers and this gorgeous stood bye, in black silk and cotton for light eyes. She shined the brightest even with mandolins on her shoulder, she walked by sitting with her legs crossed. Choirs were different but minds were alike and when I sat with her, my moon had never shone this bright.

Glaring across the three of us we landed our eyes on this violinist who spoke like the Greek sun, and the beyonding beyond he tied his arms too. He weaved the sonnets on trail of his fingers because you could see if he used his eyes we'd burn from the art. His mystic was to be aphrodite's favorite.

The set back soon sown by the fairy flute heart behind the tables of the rust, I could see her skin chevelure and her fingertips tied to her whispers. She knew that she had the burn In her and her wings never ashed. She was born from the sun, the daughter of the sky the way she ruled.

I could hear her spells repeat on the echos which cured a mist of mind, her Wand in her hand and her soul on inclined skies she condensed overwhelm the rustic in the monsoon in a brink of a letter. She had a kingdom, could possibly be our own and her name never felt shallow, felt whole.

And then there was a face in the mirror, watching across on like a stop in time. Her hair flowed like a river her jaw was shaped like a snow peak. I could say she had her head in the clouds either way but her mind was waiting to catch every lyric by her lips because she has it in her to kill the ungodly.

24. Banglore

Summertime in banaglore
While we surf at museums
Cant find a piece prettier
Than your smile
And to every artist I glance
Leonardo, Picasso Johannes
Nothing made me feel weaker
Thn the way your lips dance
And you're written along siren symphonies
Which I can read till poets lake
Each word of you is graced
With golden, silver lace
A dance along the edge to feel
A crisp along the burn
Eyes that met you unlike what I've
ever seen
Just turns me into dust
It's remorseful to even forget your name
It's a thread to be knotted
The brightness that lip cross gave me
Was never to be spoken
I've never seen a prettier smile
And I've never melted so light

Every polariad of your face
Is nothing less than a prize

25. Highschool

And she cried her eyes out for a friend who doesn't even care, a friend who probably wouldn't mind losing her. And I know she is so in love with friendships and can't let go, but today felt so intense and awfully intense today. I counted every tear that went down those eyes I admired for every day, I can see everyone so clearly yet can't help. She has been a part of my life since 8th grade even when I ignored to accept it. I realized she'd Laid her eyes on *her* the day they meet and she didn't she? I knew I was right all along. Today the grine broke her arm after she ditched her "best friend". And she cried till her eyes burnt but then was the one who ran into the fire, the fire was thrown brink of explosion and she walked in it little knowing she lost more than her arm. She lost someone who's been on friend since it all. Doesn't she regret a thing? A single thought? Is being popular more important than her friend? Who knows, ethics are weird and odd. Even then, she kept telling the masked boy how to take care of the grine and to bring an extra black pen, a bit of her favorite food, the incomplete notebooks, and all of it. She's so intense with her love it that can scar her, she reminds me of me, I wish I could show that much rage for platplatonice's just so unsown on her skies, you could fall in every bit of her.

26. Pickwickian

You know as a seeming Pickwickian I actually sondered since 3rd grade. I fail to realize how maturity is poisoned by age, I myself am still a child I shouldn't be mature enough to sonder indefinitely for others whilst they ignore my clank of existence. The consciousness that's pinching me to elaborate everyone's on their problems

27. Rubies

And she always smiled like she ran through a garden of sunflowers under the sunset but her horizon was the mind. Stuck between darkness and light trying her best to reach the stars but tied to the midlands of her own mind but she never let it show because her lisps were a language you could only understand if you followed her eyes. You could see the fog in her mind and the infinite caverns that resided in and oh how I'd love to live where she does. Caves and caves of darkness but the darkest grows the brightest and once you spark a sip of sunlight in that caves you can see the rubies.

The red in her rubies was the love she caressed but never let show, she was made of love, she was made of gardens she walked on. She was made of rubies~

28. Unfolded

And he unfolded his curtains for the first time, I was looking at a movie. His face felt like a scene so serene it could outdo the whole of titanic, a scene that was lighted by the sun and his eyes shone in the basking rays through the school window. I glanced at him as he sat in the corner of the classroom; suddenly, he was all I could glance at. waiting for him to take off his curtains to ask me to talk to him. I was envious of him, his voice, his face, his eyes, his hair. He looked perfect, he looked like he was written in a novel, and oh how I'd love to read it, to read him. His mysteries his mind his soul
I wonder what he thinks and what he likes. He's stood out forever and I wonder how long can he hold being unknown to me.

29. Ballroom

In a ballroom full of hundreds of lovers I stand between the two, a girl with a smile that mesmerized my mind and a boy with eyes with pierces my heart. Both as light and bright as the burning sun but my selene soul who am I to rival these two pollent arriviste's.

I stare down at the mirror on the marble wall asking myself "do I choose a lover who healed me forever or the one I stumbled upon as a lovesick destiny"

why am I even making a question? I should choose the girl with the sun's smile. But the boy with the sun eyes got me risen forever.

Someone who I'm to be with or someone I'm to be for?

I came to the hall as they both take my hand, time after time we switch places, and every time I meet the sun-eyed boy I feel the sunset, and every time I dance with the sun-smile girl I feel the sunrise.

The Day and night is a game of deities, a love thin rivalry to prove who can go longer without dancing to the same beat, that's what's happening with me

Why can't a moon have two suns?

Why is my heart filled with choices?

When I go to my soul runs

All I hear are indecisive voices

Help me weep across the sight
To love me as I could sworn to
The lovers who were bound by soul
And the one that soul they're bound to
Endless memories of romance
But the instability of belonging
The Choice Is in my hands
But my hands aren't enough worthy

30. Surviving

Do you know that hollow feeling of lacking something that isn't necessarily important but feels like the world to you?
Do you know how monsoon inches today but the day it doesn't rain you feel like a season lost?
Do you know how the Tenth grade always felt this deep reminisced hollow of mystery boy when he doesn't come to school for the brief 10 minutes?
You know how when your Class Teacher is absent and instead of feeling like you have more freedom you feel the discomfort of not being with someone who knows you?
You know that weird sensation you get when something is gonna go wrong but it doesn't so it lurks in the back of your mind for ages?
These moments of unidentifiable emotions constraint our time to make it feel unreal, which makes us feel Haunted from the inside out even though we know these things don't matter that much to the expanse of how much you'll live but that rainless monsoon day, Your favorite student being late, your class teacher being absent and that feeling of something going wrong? The short termed anxiety?
I feel like that's home now, that's all I've ever felt, every other emotion has been a substance inside this moment of variable time. You feel lost, and hopeless because of something small

but the next day you feel lost because of another reason. These small things make a paranoid sense and cause you to live in the unfamiliarity of everything. You're too conscious, too carefree, too focused but too tired.
You're not living You're surviving

31. You're

You're what art galleries are to artists
You're what Book stores are to Writers
You're what bakeries are to pâtissier
You're what gardens are to florists
Darling, you're where I find what I crave
But I can't stay in the hotel of your heart forever
But trust me I'll stay as long as I can
But we are kids anyway so we'll part ways
But till then.
Hold my hand and tell me it's okay
That's October isn't the end of the day
That love isn't hierath I sway
That I deserve to live another way

32. Dearanged

If I was written to be the greatest warrior of all time I wouldn't be in an asylum would I? It's precise that I'm a foster in love but in reality, my heart just won't stop destroying my own mind. Don't you hate when you can't figure out of you fell for someone from your heart or your mind, now imagine if it's both. Your heart says they'd treat you well and love you but your mind rips its tendons to get to him first, it wants you to make a web and make him fall, it wants you to snatch every inch of him.

Why? Just. Why?

Jealousy.

The whispers that say to stop and the timings are all deranged.

It's all a whimpering inch of a struggle.

He's gorgeous that's what he is, he's beautiful.

Love is thin and the mind is sharp so when they clash a war begins with yourself but for me, the war was always there, it just has more agony now.

I'm terrified to admit my love

I'm truly not proud of where I've come

I just want a home

Which isn't temporary

33. Before the beggining

Do you ever see someone and it feels like you've known them since the start of existence? Like you played in the stars when the sun wasn't ours and when you hid behind the moon because the earth wasn't cool and you tagged along valleys of galaxies unknown before you set foot on earth to distance into two? You see the scars of your past that split you in half and yet you mourn to yourself that you're complete. Soulmates are made not found but what if my soul is only as half as his? I've felt his heart too close to my own but when we are four millennials apart how close can we slow? The wild heart of mine that races on the coast to risk every fire spark that destiny has to show. The calm calm heart of his that swims across the sea to twist and turn around to avoid heat completely. I am a disguise he's preserving, I'm the guide he's the tourist, and dynamically, either way, the butterflies need flowers to sit on, and the sun needs earth

34. Pink sky

"The sky is pink"
She said as we glared across the most gorgeous sunset I could see. Sitting at a picnic cloth in her pink dress upon the corset, with the almost wolf-cut hair and an unsettling bubbly smile. She looked like the daisy fields yet again. We painted the sky with the clouds, she color them with the bubblegum we blew. Sat beside a lake clicking Polaroids with the 1976 Pentax. Who knew I'd never forget the smell of that never happening date?

Lovers don't occur to me anymore, because you can hold hands with just friends, I don't think I'd want to love her as I did to Vanilla yet I'd want to have her eyes look at me. At least to let her know I exist.

for her, with her, because of her.

35. Hellfire

The sad thing about loving heroes is you'll never meet them in the afterlife. There exists a heaven and a hell,
Every savior, save in his own story but for someone who lost their life at a war they never fought for has the savior as an ignitor.
And heroes always go to hell,
And darling you'll go to heaven for loving a sinner
You'll go to heaven for finding love for the unlovable
Maybe one day you can be the next Lucifer
And we'll be on the same plane again
With a love that burns more than hellfire.

36. Flesh

I've seen scattered flesh
Formed to love Someone unloved
With the mirage of auspicious stress
With walls of glass
It feels ripen
The soul of my bel amour
Romanticizing each word
That goes by row
Is she to steal it for safe
Will she forever be riled
Every time I see her face
I never trust my eyes
Lips so deep I can drown in her lisps
Eyes shaped like mountain lakes
The jaw of a mermaid with
contagious vocals
Feels like a sirens allure bane
Will she dance to the end of the world with me
Or will she end me with the save
Does it matter if I live for a season
When eternity has left my trails

37. September

It's September end again, the leaves will fall above my shoulders and the monsoon will weep for springs that never came, the sky burns more every October I live and I let it be because I'm too weak to Whisk the clouds. I might not live, but I don't want that to change you even tho you will. Death hurts, Losing and hurts, but I'm an alibi for tonight, tomorrow, and maybe a few weeks more. Will you remember me when your favorite leather book shines in my eye hue? I don't know. Maybe I'd rather not want to be remembered. My biggest fear was not to be remembered but in the great expanse of existence, nothing is a reality so I'd rather leave with hearts that never ached on my name than hearts that never knew me. I was too scared to touch the gold, I always wanted to be silver. I wanted to love silvers but. I drowned in Aqua Regia.

Love was always an ecstasy
And Ecstasies are always made of fantasies
And you don't deserve fantasies because they're myths
And myths are for one's who were folklore to be
And just like in most folklore, I was cursed

38. Unique

The way I molded my Insecurities into self esteem discomfort was all broken away today, while I talked to my drunk uncle at 1:00 AM he said
"you're an amazing kid, I hope you become the best poet of the generation and trust me I know you will"
and there was my usual response
"Everyone can write"
He stared at me and said
"Lekin sab Dil se nahi Likh sakte hai"
This means that not everyone can be vulnerable to heart while writing
I was too stunned to respond, I had something that made me special.
When I look at my poetry with admiration and pride I realize how much I have grown
When I look at my poetry
and when I'm sad I realize how much I can grow, my extreme potential which I can achieve somehow someday.
My broken potential needed this one sentence to rearrange itself to feel the warmth of being unique

39. Last Smoke

You told me you smoke
I Rested on the terrace
Waiting for you to sit
Along the sidelines of the schools risk
You told me you you don't care
So I lit up your cigar
And we laughed till the end of
Melodies that scar
You told me you hated your brother
I said I do too
Knowing neither of us got his love
When we really wanted to
You told me it's funny
That I fell for an idiot
I rested my head on your shoulder
Saying "don't you always too"
I know this is a time bomb
Waiting for 2023
But till the school collides us
Why can't we just be free
Wish we go to visit Cannought ace
And click blurry pictures of us
To find every Cliche you see

We find in our fate too

40. Skyline

And she felt like the sky, her skin soft like she was born in a river and her eyes looked like the sun just in the shape of a horizon. She had the earth in her, she was the purest that nature has ever created and I've never seen a girl so serene. Her smile I could write books about her lips looked like lotuses and her hair looked like rain. If I could hold her hand I'd be on a train around the world and the world has never been so pretty before I saw her.
if she had green eyes she'd be a goddess.
but I guess there is one thing that separates us from being museum piece

41. Fract

Fract of the untold voices
That is sealed within your lips
Your gilded trophies of poetry
That I've written within
The lips are sealed with seamless secrets
Can I even uncover those threads
That rearranges the kite you fly on
Maybe the forever lost will be left
And to the hell of my mind where you lie within
Just sitting there pretty and seamless
Your gorgonizing vicious eyes that
Seems like we are forever sky gazing
As I follow through your crystal mind
Which I expected to be glass
Every curve of the words you tell me
Just feels like a history class
Is it okay to be that pretty in bee
Because I've seen you with that shirt
The yellow and black striped Tee
That Sweven left on my earth
Nacreous Nights with your songs
That whilst my shadows into the aurora
With October to May ending mayhem

You've molded my orphic clover
As i leap through your songs
I sew upon a dream
An Anadem made of roses
With a little note that says "Leal

42. Fondness

The sun sets in my piercing skin, maybe not the sun but whatever it is it burns like it. The veil is in shambles and my mind is still lost to figure out what love is supposed to be for. For the pretty girl in the standard up who lightens the hallways with lips of rose, or is it for the boy at the choir who never seems to fail when it comes to being a siren on the shore? I glance across a mirror maze where my eyes land on them and yet my heart crumbles upon knowing love is for either of them. Love isn't romanced it's the fondness of my heart and yet when the glass maze breaks, the scattered Sunrays pierce this heart.

To Oliver Wilde,

To be Born to death.

And yet the Soil loves me.

With no regret.

43. Love

And then I realized perfectionism infatuated me
But it's mistakes that enable me to love
I don't fall in love with people who have their necks held on golden tables
I fall in love with people who have realized golden table isn't the destination
Because destinations don't exist when your soul is immortal
I fall in love with immortals
Because regardless of if the ever after exists
We have a bind of extravagance
To find a journey every once in eternity
This is what I call love

44. Riverside

The riverside that's destined
Upon your request for cue
And the sun glistens on the river
And our legs in the stray
Gilted hillside of our fates
I've wedged and weaved
A string of the untouched twinkle
That's been set free
Psithurism still dances in the forest
Along the lines of your acapella
And while we sit on the rocks
Revealed our legs to the flow
A tune that mascaras my eyes
With the slightest pink of your voice
A symphony that feels through
hearts
And tells me a tale of seas
The riverbeds, they're light with stars
The riverbanks, they're bright with ours
Our stories of across the guitars
Our stories across bazaars
Yet the sunset wasn't the prettiest
When I sat near the riverside

When I talk about the prettiest
It wasn't either your eyes
I saw you sing, across the forest
I heard you feel the songs of the night
And the prettiest thing I've witnessed
Is your voice at midnight

45. Satisfaction

Mastering the art of being satisfied with your life is always the worst on-edge feeling ever, while I feel so Caged to be optionless on a night when everyone else is enjoying makes it unreliable, makes it awful, makes it despising. You feel the need to shove it down the throat to be happy with what you have is a total killer statement you know why? I know I deserve better. I wanna know what it feels to party I want to know what it feels to hang out I wanna feel how it feels to make funny dance videos I wanna feel to go on dates with my best friend I wanna feel to know how the world feels around me.

I'm not wanting my heart to be Caged in my own bones.

46. Poison Orchids

The moonlight strikes me while I wait on to be someone I want to be. I have the same eyes as a fortnight ago yet every vision is in slumber and my heart is aslow.

Do you ever look at love, and think the word itself doesn't do it justice?

If you were to hunt down Bombay Beach you'd never find me in the sand. If were to count my tears You'd find me in a pond of my classmate's disguise, and how my hate for not being them kills me from within.

I assure you it be my lowest problem, to be a romance that strikes me hollow because I sit at my favorite bird Sanctuary alone.

We think so much, of whatever,

That everyone just is too tired to hold my hand, that everyone is sleeping in their cozy hobbit houses.

But they just dislike my honeydew collection since my win at the choir means nothing, since my trip to the sun and back didn't almost burn me.

That swallowtail will never remember the poison orchids.

47. Insanity

It's been a while since I woke up this early, rather I didn't sleep at all.

I just woke up from the thoughts that conquered my esteem to finish off the Moon bird for once and for all, I waited to see how long would it take for a knife to slice open every wing in half but the moon stayed octennial worlds away. The birds that chirped were poisoned by the sun and the summer clouds' rains despair but the silver Selene stayed at the night. Covered away in eternal winter that feeds it to be such a pearl that if you put it In a clam the clam swallows all the 7 seas. The frigus beast stays on the midnight orb, why doesn't It help?

The part of me that's connected to the moonlight crest is freezing while the summer sun burns off my skin. I'm in a war with two Supremes that cannot be fixed with logistics because they comprehend four risks greater than that of mere mortals such as I. A fight between the forevers where the citation of a word in this book of infinity never rhymes. Maybe my poetry will end within the concept of my insanity

48. Sundown

So when sundown starts
And my mind is flooded with memories
Of what could've been instead of
What has been, I remind myself
Day after day that
I've longed for this week
The summers when I'm finally free
The summer of the '20s
Every deranged thought is just
Useless, as useless as it can be
Every smear of light that runs across
My red, freckle cheeks
I'm so tired of wanting to survive
Because I've never felt like to live
And as I sit down here writing poetry
I know some of you can probably relate
And the nights of the days
My eyes were swollen because of reasons
Sad, bliss, reeking, serve, unreal
Yet realistically none of those matter
The paper with ABCs
And all the seven seas

And the vigorous growth of vines
That makes my heartbeat leak
I'm covered with blood
Is it admiration? Is it dissociation?
I don't know
I just feel myself burning to survive
But I wanna learn to live

49. Constellations

You're so lost in songs while watching you hum the tunes of guitars you never picked up over the boys who made you swoon over. beside you at our bedframe, staring across those eyes thinking how he loves the stars. His obsession with astrology is so much more than zodiacs. He loves the skies; ironically, I see it in his eyes because those bronze eyes have more than the copper sea in them. I love how he looks at me because he never does, he looks away at every glance. ***Nazarien churana to koi isse sikhe***. And you'll never understand how inviting those blooming lips are, that sweet face and that blush. He scribbles down a picture of my glasses at the side of his notebook page, maybe he's in love too, and maybe I'd be able to make a constellation of ink in his memory.

While we wink from different corners of the room we know our minds are mirrors of mystique.

50. Every star

And I whist to the sky the tiniest of secrets I realize the stories made from my memories are worth every gilded coin. I know when the sun goes down my secrets are safe with the azure and when the moon shines on me I can see myself shining bright. People carry dairies and journals to write their secrets on the prettiest pages with the lightest pens with the brightest inks but I just write my stories in the sky with clouds and mists.
A thing I'm fascinated by is how my secrets float in the air in waves
anyone could hear yet no one finds them, I could lay in the spot for hours to remember all the words I said like a book of the sky and it just runs along with my lips Because every word I speak is as gorgonizing as the sky.
The more I speak the more I gather the views of the world and the sky has a million secrets, it talks in hints, It gives me wisdom in the most beautiful reminiscence you could feel.
The sky doesn't care what you do, or who you love because the sky is made of you, It's been with you It's been in you, it's been on you. It of you. The
sky sees you.
The sun is the eyes The moon and the portal.
the air a cradle.
and the ground a mirror.

You are worth every star you can count on a clear night.

9 798888 692486

Printed by Libri Plureos GmbH in Hamburg, Germany